AF364712

MANGAL MEDIA

Evliya Çelebi Mah. Sadi Konuralp Cad. IKSV Vakfı
No:5 Iç Kapı no:2 Beyoglu / Istanbul
Turkey

Writer
Zymolust Ravenson

Artist
Zezeah

Book Design
Feyza Daloglu & Efe Levent

From the Dark, Zymolust Ravenson & Zezeah, 2023

ISBN 978-605-70348-9-2

© Mangal Media, 2023, Istanbul

FROM THE DARK

by

Zymolust Ravenson

&

Zezeah

CONTENTS

Part I. From the Dark (2005)

Air Force Intelligence Directory

click

TV comes on

"...he became prime minister for the first time in 1992. He is a rare case of a Lebanese leader who has not fought in the war. He led the efforts to rebuild Beirut, particularly the downtown area. Twenty-one people were killed in addition to Hariri by a blast of 1,000 kg of TNT detonated in Beirut outside the St. George Hotel. The victims included Hariri's bodyguards, and ..."

coffee spills

Rafic Hariri, the former Prime Minister of Lebanon, was assassinated on February 14, 2005, in a car bombing in Beirut. The assassination triggered the Cedar Revolution, a popular movement which forced Syria to withdraw all its troops in Lebanon by April 2005.

The Special Tribunal for Lebanon (STL), an international court established to investigate the assassination, found that Salim Ayyash, a member of the Lebanese Hezbollah, was the mastermind of the attack. Ayyash was killed in Syria in 2016, and the STL has not been able to bring him to justice.

The STL also found that the assassination was carried out with the support of the Syrian government and the Iranian government.

OLYMPICS: CA

There's a lot of excitement Olympics are coming to Hackr London in just seven years ti

asks

...inking this. ...earning Trust ...gerston School, ...ut to ask people ...vey carried out ...e and July, we' ...ed the Council's

...t trying to force ...hool on us? It is ...with privatising ... rid of their ...g from running ...g our estates. ...d our estate ...shift the whole ...LMO company. ...g of our schools ...now they want ...hey can to City ...d transferring ...cil is their one

...s guinea pigs in ...tion since they ...his time it is not ...kids, it is about ...e support the ...pupils and staff ...nd Shoreditch ...opposing the ...banner in our ...erston"!

IA

What the fuck?

It's February 2005 and while the entire Middle East is going into darkness, I just finished work on my album: From the Dark.

Sometime in March 2005

Me: Ok guys I'm going home now.

My friend: Cool, take care, man. I just wanna say one more time, I really loved your album. It's everything it says on the tin.

Me: I'm glad you like it. I was a little worried about the recording quality.

It's almost as though I used a washing machine to record instead of a decent computer.

My friend: *laughing* yea it is totally fine bro. You must not forget you did everything by yourself, no one helped you except with words. You can re-record it in the future when you get better equipment.

Me: Yea... but it's the moment, you know... each and every album or track has its own soul. They all sound different each time I play them. It's like they can sense my feelings, thoughts, heart, everything...

My friend: It's like they say: You can't step in the same river twice.

Me: Damn right! Well, anyway. See you.

Walking around at 11 pm through mostly empty streets is not scary. Its actually quite nice. Peaceful, somehow. Just empty wet streets. There is something beautiful about streets being wet. Beautiful cold breeze, there are some cats taking shelter under cars and sleeping dogs.

Suddenly the security services white Peugeot 505 appears from the corner... And I hear my inner voice speak.

-Excuse me?!
-You're excused.
-What the...!
-Oh my fuck!
-Did you just say "White Peugeot...

-I knew it!
-Maybe it's not them?
-Who else is going to shout like this
at this time in Tartus?
-Yea… Well…

Oky, it's official…

Two agents are coming toward me from
that damn car.
France! I will never forgive you! They are
holding two AK-47s and they look very
angry for some reason.

Agent 1: (With Bedouin accent): You! Who are you?

Me: I'm just going home. I live here.

Agent 1: What home?

Me: My home?

Agent 2: (With an Alawi accent) I never saw you before!

Me: I never saw you before.

Agent 1: I passed by this street ten minutes ago but didn't see you.

Me: Yes exactly! I was not here ten minutes ago, I was coming...

Agent 2: What???

Me: I mean I didn't reach this street ten minutes ago, because I was walking and walking and walking for ten minutes and here I am after ten minutes, which is now!

Agent 1: Give me your damn ID, you idiot!

-Ok Salem, listen to me!
-Shut. The. Fuck. Up! We're fucked!
-Not necessarily man, we can...
-No! We can't.
-We can't what?
-We can't anything!
-Yea, well, you're probably right..
Ok, let's do as he says!
-As if we have another option.

I hand over my ID. Agent 1 checks my ID while Agent 2 is searching me for weapons.

Agent 1: What is this?

Me: It's my ID.

Agent 1: What kind of ID is this?

Agent 2: Show me!

Agent 1: here.

I know exactly what's going to come next. Here we go: 3... 2... 1...

Agent 2: What is this? Are you Lebanese??

Me: Well...Yes, I happen to be Lebanese.

Agent 1: Lebanese?? Let me see this ID. You're Lebanese?

Me: Yes, yes, I am Lebanese. I swear I'm Lebanese. Wallah, I'm Lebanese.

Agent 1: What are you doing here?

Me: I was walking until you stopped me. Now I'm talking to you guys.

Agent 1: I mean what are you doing here, in Tartus!

Me: I live here.

Agent 1: How?

Agent 2: Where is your visa?

Me: What visa?

Agent 2: How did you enter our country?

Me: Using the ID in your hand.

Agent 2: You entered without a visa? Illegally?

What kind of "intelligence" agent doesn't know that Syrians and Lebanese can enter each others' country without an ID?

Me: No, I live here. Just a few...

Agent 2 to Agent 1: Get this idiot!

Agent 1: Walk!

Me: Are you arresting all Lebanese?

Both: Shut up!

Here I am in this beautiful car for the first time.
I'm sitting in the back between these two morons.

Driver: Who is that son of a ****

Agent 1: We caught a Lebanese!

Caught? Like I was jumping from tree to tree in the forest and they trapped me?

Driver: Lebanese? What the hell is a Lebanese doing here?

Me: I live here, people!

Driver: You live here in the middle of the night?

Me: I also live here in the morning!!!

Agent 2: *Hits me with the butt of his rifle* Don't speak smartass!

Me: Ok!

Agent 1: *Hits me with the butt of his rifle* He told you not to say a word!

Me: Actually, he told me not to speak I jus...

Agent 2: *Hits me with his elbow* We ordered you to shut the fuck up!

Me: *with a weak voice* Ok! Ok! Got it!

Agent 1: Shut up!

Me: *nodding my head*

Agent 1: Don't move your ugly head!

- Ugly? I never heard of an "ugly" head! I think heads are big or small. How the hell can a head be ugly? Maybe it's a cultural thing. Who knows. Do they call smart people "beautiful heads"?
- For fuck sake Salem, what are you thinking about now?
- It's a very weird adjective, man.
- You are being taken by unknown agents who work for an unknown security intelligence department, and no one knows about you being taken!
- Yeah but, man! Ugly head?
- I know, yeah, I'll give you that. It's pretty weird. We never heard of that.
- Right?
- Yea.
- So what did he mean by...
- SALEM!
- Ok ok ok, focus!

We are now entering some headquarters. No name, no sign, no idea what the hell it is

Agent 1: Get out you animal!

slap

Agent 1: Stand still, hands on your back *puts handcuffs on*.

I'm in a room after a hard kick, it's dark and it smells very very bad.

A whispering voice in the dark: Hey

Me: Bismillah!! What the fuck!

Voice: Shhh don't be loud!

Me: What are you?

Same voice: I'm human.

Me: No kiddin' I know you're a goddamn human. I meant who are you? What's going on here?

Voice: Are you Jordanian?

Me: No, I'm not! Why? Are they arresting Jordanians as well? Are you Jordanian?

Voice: No! I'm Palestinian.

Me: Ok? What's going on?

Palestinian guy: There was a Jordanian guy before you.

Me: Are they collecting the Arab League here? What do they want from you?

Palestinian guy: They were interrogating me about some stereo.

Me: Stereo? What are you talking about, man? Look I don't wanna know. Just tell me where the hell are we?

Palestinian guy: You don't know?

Me: I do know. I'm just asking for a laugh. Answer the damn question!

Palestinian guy: Ok, ok, it's the Air Force Intelligence Directory.

Me: What the fuckin' fuck?! Air Force Intelligence?!

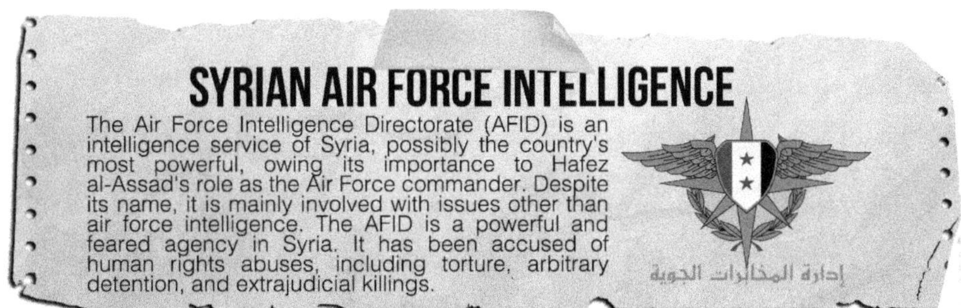

SYRIAN AIR FORCE INTELLIGENCE

The Air Force Intelligence Directorate (AFID) is an intelligence service of Syria, possibly the country's most powerful, owing its importance to Hafez al-Assad's role as the Air Force commander. Despite its name, it is mainly involved with issues other than air force intelligence. The AFID is a powerful and feared agency in Syria. It has been accused of human rights abuses, including torture, arbitrary detention, and extrajudicial killings.

إدارة المخابرات الجوية

Welcome to one of the country's most powerful and dreadful directories, owing its importance to Hafez Assad's role as the air force commander. Despite its name, it is mainly involved with issues that have nothing to do with the Air Force. They took an active part in the suppression of the Muslim Brotherhood rebellion in the

Election Result

1982 HAMA MASSACRE

The Hama massacre was a massacre that took place in February 1982, when the Syrian Arab Army and the Defense Companies, under orders of president Hafez al-Assad, besieged the town of Hama for 27 days in order to quell an uprising by the Muslim Brotherhood against the Ba'athist government. The campaign that had begun in 1976 by Sunni Muslim groups, including the Muslim Brotherhood, was brutally crushed in an anti-Sunni massacre at Hama, carried out by the Syrian Arab Army and Alawite militias under commanding General Rifaat al-Assad.

The exact number of people killed in the Hama massacre is unknown, but estimates range from 10,000 to 25,000. It has been described as a genocide by some human rights groups. The United Nations Human Rights Commission condemned the massacre, and the European Parliament called for an international investigation.

1980s. Anyone who knows anything about what's going on in Syria is guaranteed to piss themselves as soon as they hear that name said out loud.

Palestinian guy: Yes, It's a...

Me: Shhh don't be loud!

Palestinian guy: ??? I'm not lou...

Me: Shut up! Don't talk to me! Actually, don't talk at all!

Palestinian guy: But I...

Me: Shut up! Shut up! Not a word! No words! No hand motions! No blinks!

Palestinian guy: It's dark, man!

Me: Ummm!

- Congratulations Salem! You made it!
- Thank you... now you shut the fuck up too.
- What an idiot
- I was walking down the goddamn street! Is this a crime?!
- It is in Syria. Especially it you're a Lebanese, moron.
- Some big help you are, inner voice!
- Well it I am, then so are you!

Fuck you, and fuck Salem.
-We got two fucks between the two
of us. One for you and one for me.
-Aren't you forgetting one?
-Which one?
-You didn't count the fucking we are
about to get from the Air Force In-
telligence!
-Amazing! Thanks for keeping count.

Palestinian guy: Hey

Me: ...

Palestinian guy: Yo dude!

Me: ...

Palestinian guy: You still there?

Me: No, I evaporated! Yes, I'm still here, what do you want?

Palestinian guy: What are you here for?

Me: Tourism!

Palestinian guy: What?

Me: I got caught by these people, what do you expect?

Palestinian guy: No. I mean why?

Me: It's because of a CD player.

Palestinian guy: What? It doesn't make sense.

Me: Would it make more sense if it were a stereo?

Palestinian guy: That's your crime? Impossible.

Me: It would be impossible if this were Scotland Yard.

Palestinian guy: What? What is that?

Me: Ugh... Never mind.

Palestinian guy: Tell me.

Me: It's a football team! Now shut up, please!

the iron door opens

Jailer: Zymolust Ravenson!

Me: Yes!

Jailer: come here, you idiot!

I am taken to another room for interrogation. Handcuffed, blindfolded and on my
knees.

Interrogator: Your name!

Me: My name is...

-Slim Shady, yes I'm
the real Shady
-What the fuck? Now is
not the time, inner voice!
-Ok ok

Interrogator: You forgot your name? You animal!!!

Me: It's Zymolu...

Interrogator: Shut the fuck up!!!

kicks me in the stomach

What a pain... It's like my guts want
to leave my body. It's really a kick.
They are not just punching no more. It's
getting serious now.

Interrogator: What is your name, bitch!

Me: Zymolust S. Ravenson, sir!

kicks me on the shoulder

Interrogator: I did not allow you to answer!

Me:...

Interrogator: Answer!

slap

Me: Zymolust S. Ravenson, sir!

spits on my face

Interrogator: Disgusting name! Where are you from, you piece of shit?

Me: I'm from Tartous, sir.

Interrogator: Are you fucking lying to me?!

And there are lots of kicks, hits,
punches and swearings of course. Not to
mention using my long hair as a handle

to make sure I won't hide my face. I really didn't have to walk through that street. What a crazy idea that was. I could've just walked through the one behind it. There would also be cats and dogs and wet streets! It is so embarrassing to be insulted like this. It is embarrassing to watch myself in this situation. Although no one I know will ever see what's happening here, it will still be in my memory forever. The only one who will ever know is this interrogator. It breaks something inside a person. Your dignity tries to hold on as tight as possible, your inner self tries to stand as long as possible. But eventually, there will always be a breaking point.

I now hate every street in this city, wet or dry, with or without cats!

Interrogator: Enough!

Yea. enough, I'm so ready. I'm ready to confess to assassinating J. F. K.

Interrogator: Now answer, where are you from and who sent you?

Me: I'm Lebanese, but I live in Tartus.

Interrogator: Listen, for every lie you say we will fuck your God!

-What? Does he listen to Deicide?
-Nah, That's impossible...

Me: Yes.

Interrogator: When was the last time you've been to Lebanon?

Me: 2003.

Interrogator: What were you doing?

Me: I was finishing my military service.

Interrogator: Which army?

Me: Lebanese Army

Interrogator: You think you have a real army? You are all nothing but gays and sissies.

Me: Yes, sir.

Interrogator: You are a spy!

Me: No, no, sir! I'm...

Interrogator: Shut up, animal!

Me: ...

Interrogator: Tell me how you're working for the Lebanese intelligence and what you are spying on.

Me: No...

Interrogator: Shut up!

slap

Interrogator: You are a spy, and you're spying for the Lebanese on the Syrian military!

What fuckin' Syrian military? I don't even give a single fuck about the whole region. I just want to get the fuck out of Syria and Lebanon. These are not my countries! I would rather live on the north pole. Fucking spy... what is there to spy on? And for who? All of you will go to a very, very special place in hell.

Me: Sir, I lived my whole life in Syria, I know nothing about Lebanon, and...

Interrogator: Your ID says you're a terrorist!

A spy for the Lebanese, and a terrorist? What a mix. All written on my ID, no less. How come, moron?

Me: How come, sir?

Interrogator: Your ID says you're from Tripoli!

Me: Yes, sir.

Interrogator: Tripoli is the source of terrorists!

Oh yea, I'm Sunni. Goddammit! I'm not only Lebanese, I'm also Sunni! I must be Satan himself. Shoot me in the head!

Interrogator: You must be shot in the head!

What the...? He can hear me? Hey! Can you hear me, chump?

Interrogator: We are not chumps you know. We know you have agents working with you across Syria. A web of spies!

Me: No, sir! Not at all!

Interrogator: Do you want the Syrian army to withdraw from Lebanon?

Aha! Now I get it! You lowlife, you motherfucking pieces of shit!

They are punishing Lebanon by random-ly arresting Lebanese nationals. It must be their response to the Cedar Revolution protests against the assassination of the Lebanese Prime Minister and the support of the international community for the

CEDAR REVOLUTION

The Cedar Revolution, also known as the Independence Uprising, was a series of peaceful demonstrations that took place in Lebanon from February 14 to April 25, 2005. The protests were sparked by the assassination of former Prime Minister Rafik Hariri, and they called for the withdrawal of Syrian troops

The Cedar Revolution was a major turning point in Lebanese history. It led to the withdrawal of Syrian troops from Lebanon, which had been occupying the country for 29 years. Syrian troops withdrew from Lebanon in April 2005.

withdrawal of Syrian troops from Lebanon.
I really don't give a fuck about none of
these games or political wars! Only a regime like this one would recruit others for
their filthy wars.

Me: No, no, sir! Syrians should stay in Lebanon forever!
Interrogator: Forever?
Me: Forever, sir!
Interrogator: Why?

Why indeed...

Me: Because, the Syrian regime...
Interrogator: Regime?

Wtf Salem!

Me: Because Syria is the only country in the world that can maintain peace
and security in a chaotic country like Lebanon. Lebanese are not capable of
ruling their country! They need a "big brother... like the great country of
Syria. Only Syria can play that role!
Interrogator: Aha. Go on. What else?

Isn't that enough, dumbass?!

Me: Well, there are a lot of reasons, sir.
Interrogator: Like what?
Me: I know nothing about politics, sir. All I know is that Syria should stay in
Lebanon forever! Forever!
Interrogator: Not only that, but we should also stay and rape your women!
Me:...
Interrogator: Answer!
Me: What exactly is the question, sir?
Interrogator: Say: "Yes, it's an honour for our women to be raped by the great
Syrian Arab Army...
Me:...
Interrogator: Say it!
Me: I think that the Great Syrian Arab Army is a noble army, surely they don't
act this way?

Interrogator: The Syrian Arab Army will rape you, kill you and fuck your God and still be noble! you bastard!

slap

Interrogator: Do you understand?
Me: I do understand.

I totally understand how you lowlives think. And I understand Hafez Assad and the legacy he left behind, so he would be cursed by all humanity throughout history.

Interrogator: Ali! Take this animal back to the room!

Back in the stinking room... this time alone, I don't know where that Palestinian guy is.
Maybe it's better this way. I know what that interrogator said is all bullshit to scare prisoners. Frightening people seems to be the only policy that the Syrian regime has. They are so obviously full of shit and they know it.

I'm so tired, I really need to sleep. I wish I could sleep. The only nice thing in this room is darkness. I think it's around 4 am or so. It's silent, the bastards are probably taking a rest now.

I always thought that darkness is neither scary nor evil. It should be embraced. It's funny how I kept talking about embracing darkness, but never really understood what it meant until today. Now I understand that Darkness is the only cure to all this pain and swearing against my God, my family and me. This disgusting smell, these evil people. I am watching dictatorship manifest itself in people right in front of me, turning them into monstrous beings. The nonsense, the illogical events, the ignorance. I can throw all of them into the darkness. At least for a few minutes, I can give my broken self a break... Embracing the dark for humans is like returning to the first moments in a mother's womb... a human needs darkness to be whole. Darkness is never an enemy, it's a part of life. It's the origin of life, the beginning. For before light, there was darkness.

iron door opens

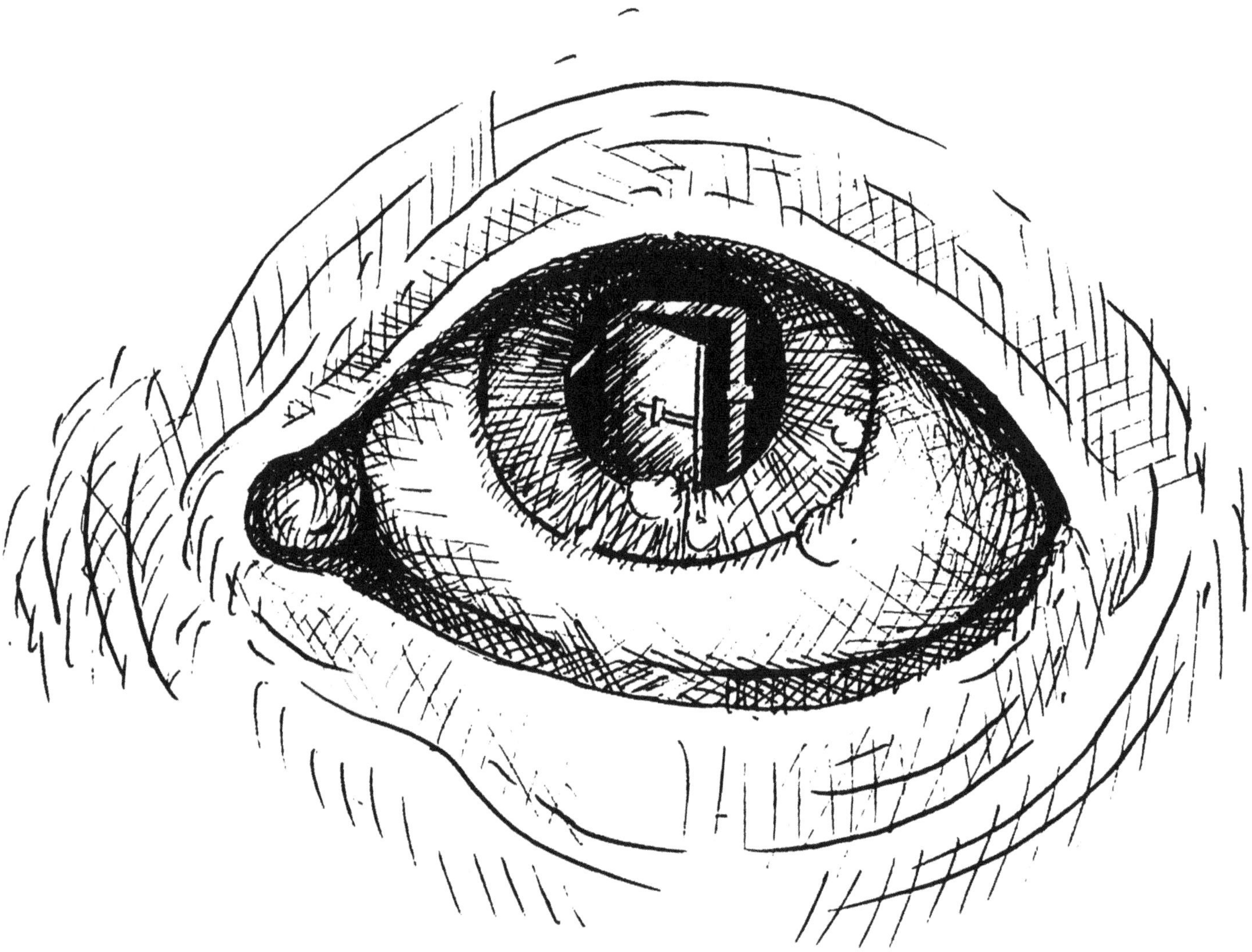

Jailer: Hey animal! Come over here.

> I am released as randomly as I was ar-
> rested. For what, no one knows, not even
> them. It is hell. No one will ever be
> safe even in their own house. There are
> no laws. A country ruled by a bunch
> of brutes with lots of weapons. There is
> no place for dialogue of any kind. All of
> this is going to blow up soon, very soon...
>
> I am Walking at dawn, heading home.
> it is as beautiful as the last time I
> was out, six or seven hours ago. But I
> just can't enjoy it anymore, it has be-
> come meaningless since last night. I just
> learned how cheap and worthless a hu-
> man being is in this land. It makes
> everything that was made for humans
> also cheap and worthless. I am think-
> ing about the things the interrogator said,
> about that dark room, the whole journey
> until I met my brother...

Brother: Where have you been, bro?

Me: I'm not sure.

Brother: I don't understand.

Me: You won't believe it.

Brother: Try me.

Me: I just came From the Dark.

Part II. Islamic Satan! (2007)
Military Intelligence

It's 2007. My uncle calls, which he never does unless some serious shit has gone down.

Uncle: Two military intelligence servicemen inquired about you this morning.

Me: Lovely. What is it this time?

Uncle: Are you asking me? Have you looked at yourself in the mirror lately? They want you to be at their HQ at 8 am sharp! I greased those two agents so they won't be making a scene at your parent's house.

Me: Sure?

I am trying to think of what it is that I'd done when the phone suddenly rings. It's my mother, with an elegy for a martyr interlaced with accusations that I am a disobedient citizen. She also gives me a piece of her mind about how I don't wear my hair the accepted length and have clothes in acceptable colours.

Me: Don't worry Mom, they won't arrest me from our house. I don't think it's a big deal, it's just a small interrogation obviously.

That makes her feel a little better.

I didn't really sleep all night. Don't really know why I am so worried since there is nothing to be worried about. EX-CEPT that I'm going to the goddamn Syrian military intelligence! In the morning I am preparing for a crisis. I choose the lamest clothes I could find in my closet and take the first cab.

Me: To the Military Intelligence HQ,

please.

Driver: I beg your pardon?

Me: Military intelligence HQ,

please?

Driver: Aha.

Me: Yea...

Driver: What a morning, ha?

Me: Yea, fantastic mornin' indeed.

MILITARY INTELLIGENCE DIRECTORATE

The Syrian Military Intelligence Directorate (SMID) is one of the most powerful intelligence agencies in Syria. It is responsible for collecting and analyzing intelligence on military threats to the Syrian government, as well as conducting covert operations in support of the Syrian military. The SMID was founded in 1969 and is headquartered in Damascus, Syria. It is headed by a general who is appointed by the President of Syria. The SMID is a secretive agency and it is difficult to get accurate information about its activities. It spends much of its resources monitoring sentiment among young Syrians and quell any social movements that might represent a threat.

I arrive at the gate of that ungodly building, where two ungodly guards are standing with guns and demonic faces.

Me (with a very fake smile): Good morning!

Guard 1: What do you want?!

Me: I'm wanted by you guys!

Guard 1: What's your damn name? Give me your ID.

Me: (Gosh this is only the entrance. Imagine what will happen inside)

Guard 2: Have you got a phone on you?

Me: I do.

Guard 2: Turn it off and hand it to me, Now!

(I do as ordered)

Guard 2: Do you have a gun on you?

Me: No no, of course I don't.

Guard 2: I'll search you! If I find a gun on you, you know what will happen!

Me: Please, go ahead and search me. I promise I don't have a gun.

He searches me as though he just arrested a terrorist but finds no gun. They let me into the building. I go into a room where Sergeant Kenan is waiting for me.

Me: Would you please explain to me why I'm wanted?

Sergeant Kenan: Actually, I already told your uncle. You were reported by high-ranking state officials.

Me: High? Ranks? A report?!

Sergeant Kenan: Yes!

Me: What is it about? What am I accused of?

Sergeant Kenan: You're accused of conducting Satanic rituals, sorcery and blasphemy. Also communicating with and working for freemasons and having a political benefit from zionist organizations!

Me: What the...? Is that real? Is that what is written in the report?

Sergeant Kenan: Yes!

Me: What does "political benefit from zionist organizations" mean?

Sergeant Kenan: Now look, be frank with me.

Me: Frank?

Sergeant Kenan: Be honest with me.

Me: Okay?

Sergeant Kenan: Do you communicate with any foreign organizations over the Internet? Do they finance you? Look, I promise you, no one will touch you. All you have to do is to confess and everything will be ok. Don't worry.

Me: Confess what, Captain Kenan?

Sergeant Kenan: It's Sergeant Kenan.

Me: Sergeant Kenan, what zionist organization are you talking about? I don't have anything to do with organizations or politics.

Sergeant Kenan: Anyway, you will be interrogated by the colonel, the deputy of the military intelligence department.

Me: Deputy?

gulp

Me: Colonel?

gulp

Sergeant Kenan: Yep!

Me: I swear I have nothing to do with that, Major Kenan

Sergeant Kenan: It's Sergeant Kenan!

Me: Sergeant Kenan. I don't want you guys to waste your time with such a small person like me. Your time is precious.

Sergeant Kenan: Don't worry, this interrogation will only take half an hour at most.

Me: Okay fine, Inshallah.

I am taken to another room. I wait
for about 40 minutes. A very thin man
comes inside. He is about 50 years old. I
stand up, he sits down then orders me
to sit. I smile stupidly. I have decided to be as stupid as possible. They feel
safe if a person is a total moron. I just
wonder what Military Intelligence has to
do with metal music, hair length, and
clothes. If Military Intelligence has become the arbiter of musical taste, does
that make the local council, for example,
responsible for diplomatic affairs? It's a
madhouse.

The Deputy starts the interrogation:

Deputy: Tell me about yourself. Do you have any hobbies? What do you do in
life?

Me: Well, actually... I'm an artist; a musician. I also like reading and pyrog-
raphy

Deputy: What kind of books do you read?

Me: Stories from English and world literature.

Deputy: Do you read political books?

Me: No, no, no! I don't know the first thing about politics, I don't like it, I
don't read about it.

Deputy: So, have you read Machiavelli's The Prince? Or books about religion
for example?

Me: (Oh how very well read.)

No, I'm of the opinion that "Religion belongs

to God and the Land belongs to all humans."

Deputy: Okay then, tell me about the music.

Me: Music is such a refined art form.

I personally think...

Deputy: *interrupts* I mean tell me about

the music you practice.

Me: Well, Mr. General-

Deputy: Colonel-

Me: Mr. Colonel, I don't discriminate. Music has no nationality.

Deputy: Okay, tell me about Satan, then.

Me: Satan?

Deputy: The devil, Lucifer, yes.

Me: What about her... him... I mean them?! It?... Maybe?

Deputy: How do you picture the devil?

Me: Well, as an artist, I picture a funny caricature...

Deputy: I hate to break it to you son, but satan is a lot uglier than that.

Me: ... Okay?

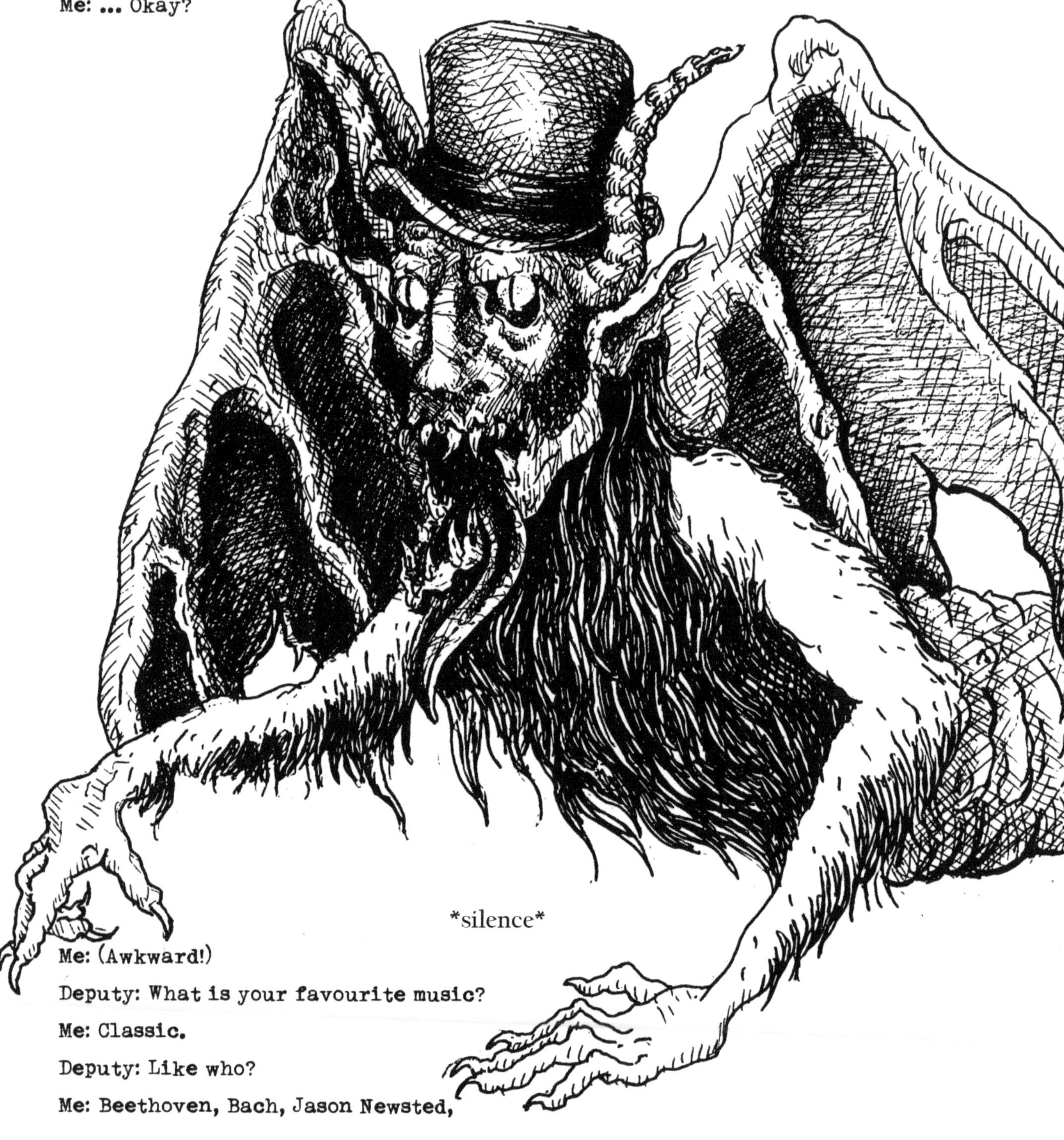

Me: (Awkward!)

Deputy: What is your favourite music?

Me: Classic.

Deputy: Like who?

Me: Beethoven, Bach, Jason Newsted,

Jonathan Davis, Abbath Doom Occulta.

Deputy: Oh, so classic.

Me: Precisely.

Deputy: Are you trying to make a fool out of me? How come you listen to classic music when you're dressed like Satanists and devil worshipers?

Me: Well, Major-

Deputy: Colonel

Me: Colonel, It's so absurd to walk around wearing Victorian clothes to reflect my musical tastes.

Deputy: Right.

Me: Right.

Deputy: So why do you dress this way?

Me: Well, since I'm an artist, I follow fashion, and these days fashion is as such.

Deputy: Ok, why do you wear your hair long? That's a Satanic ritual.

Me: (Syria's finest, mashallah) Mr. Deputy, the two are not mutually exclusive. Any artist, say a sculptor, might wear their hair long, but I don't see such foreign labels attached to them.

Deputy: What is your room like?

Me: My room?

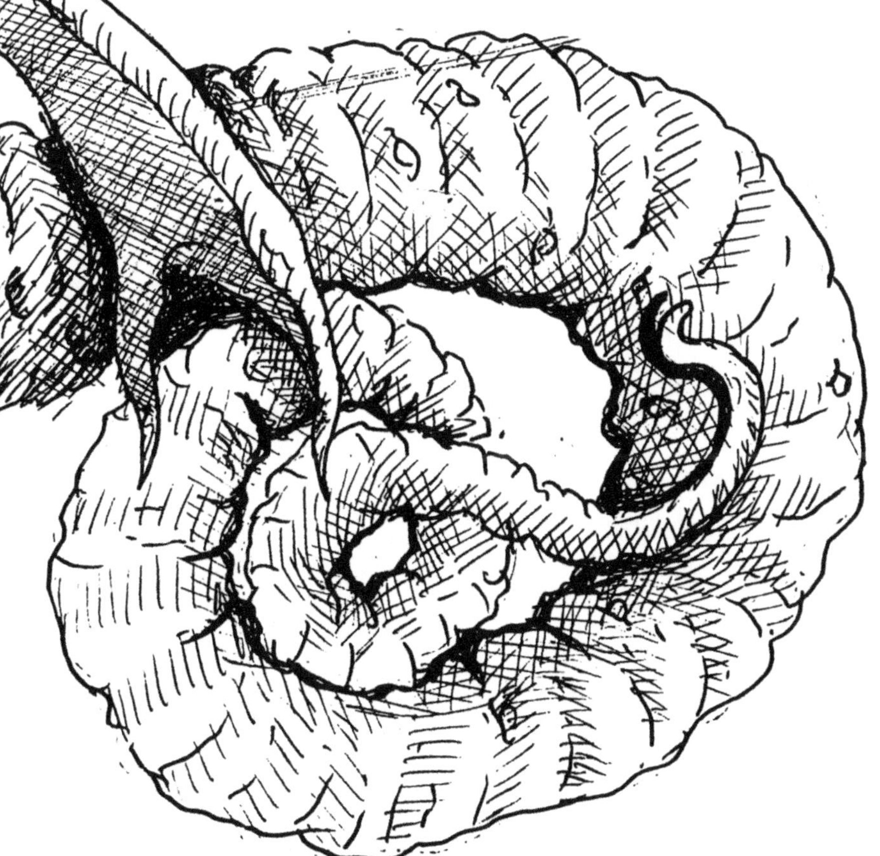

Deputy: Your room.

Me: As in my room at home?

Deputy: Are you being funny?

Me: No, no. Umm... it's just a room. What do you mean what is it like?

Deputy: Tell me what is in it?!

Me: A bed, a closet, a few shelves. Just like any old regular room.

Deputy: That's all?

Me: Oh, I also have a desk.

Deputy: Don't you keep skulls, skeletons, and corpses?

Of course... I also turn into a bat at night!

Me: God forbid. That sounds more like a morgue than a room. That's all fake news, deputy. Besides, my parents are religious people, they'd disown me if I were to do such things.

Deputy: Indeed. So do you have a modern guitar that runs on electricity?

Watch out Salem! He's a dinosaur!

Me: An electric guitar, yes.

Deputy: So you admit it!

Me: Umm... yes?

Deputy: But you just said you like classical music.

Me: I play several types of guitar.

Deputy: Why is this extravagance?

Me: Well sir, as an artist I can't sit still like a rock. I need to keep up with all the instruments and styles out there.

Deputy: True, true.

Phew...

Deputy: Do you have a computer?

Me: Yes, of course, I do. Everyone does since the great president started "the march of modernisation and development".

Deputy: That's right. What kind of music have you got on that Computer?!

Me: All kinds of music.

Deputy: Yes, what kind?

Me: All kinds, literally.

Deputy: Do you have this organization... Metalika.

Me: Metallica?! The band? I do, yes.

Deputy: You do?!

Me: Yes.

Deputy: On your personal computer?!

Me: Yes?

Deputy: And you're admitting to it? Just like that!

Me: Yes.

pause

Me: Mr. General?

Deputy: Colonel.

Me: Mr. Colonel. it's just another kind of art and as an artist, I should be aware of all kinds of music. Instead of refusing it, we should take it in. Keep your friends close but your enemies closer.

Deputy: I see.

I smile like an idiot.

Deputy: So do you... enter the internet?

Me: I'm going to be honest, I actually do.

Deputy: Where do you go on the internet? Who do you talk to?

How about I give you my girlfriend's number?

Me: Music, arts and so on.

Deputy: Do you **enter chat rooms**?

Me: Occasionally.

Deputy: What do you talk about?

Me: Music.

Deputy: Are there religious rooms?

Me: Yes.

- Noooooooooo! Saleeeeeem!!!

Deputy: RELIGIOUS ROOMS!!! ISLAMIC ROOMS?!!! YOU SPEAK TO OSAMA BIN LADEN!!!

Me: Umm... No no no, I think you got it wrong...

Deputy: (interrupting) You must tell me, now, who is your point of contact with al-Qaeda?

- That escalated quickly
- Good luck getting out of this one...
Have a nice life.
- WTF! Inner voice! Hey! Get back here!
- Thank you. But no, thank you.

Me: Allow me to clarify a thing or two about these rooms. They might be called "religious", but what goes on inside, is not at all...

Deputy: You must tell everything now! Who do you speak to? Where are they in the world? What kind of people are they, and what do you talk about? Now!

Me: I have friends from all over the world. Sir.

Deputy: Where from?

Me: All the world, literally.

Deputy: Do you talk with people from Saudi Arabia?

Shit! If I say yes, I'll be charged with terrorism.

Me: No I don't.

Deputy: Do you talk to people from Yemen?

Shit! The Houthis!

Me: No...

Deputy: How about Iraq?

This keeps getting worse...

Me: No, no.

Deputy: America?

Me: Nope.

Deputy: I thought you should keep your enemies closer.

Me: Mr. Marshall...

Deputy: Colonel.

Me: Mr. Colonel. Our people are way more advanced than these crackers. But you know, people watch those Hollywood movies and they believe all the propaganda.

Deputy: You just said you speak to people all over the world. Now it seems like you don't speak to anyone!

Me: Listen, sir, I'll be honest with you. With no offence to our Arab brothers, but I don't really like to engage with them. They only talk about politics and porn.

Deputy: Porn as in sex?

Me: Sex?

Deputy: Sex.

Sex?

Me:

silence

Deputy: SEX?

Sex?!

Me: sex?!

Deputy: YES! DO YOU TALK ABOUT SEX?!

Me: Well as an artist, I approach sex with a more refined...

Deputy: Are you sure you don't speak to al-Qaeda?

Me: Mr. Colonel, al-qaeda.com is out there on the internet. I could just go and speak to them, but I never have!

Deputy: Fine, let me ask you something else. What do you think of the internet?

-Very relevant indeed.
-Do Something.
-What the hell do I say to this idiot?
-Just Do it!
-Nike!
-SALEM!
-Ok, ok.

Me: Well, we still don't understand the internet. We must be aware that our enemies lurk in the dark waiting to destroy us. They are envious of the achievements of our new Syria and our president Bashar Al Assad, may God Protect him. But I assure you sir, this country is guarded against their ill-intention by a divine will.
Deputy: Exactly!
Me: I'm telling you, sir!
Deputy: Well, it is obvious that you are a person who knows our enemy and you're aware of the conspiracies and plots against our defiant country.
Me: Absolutely, Mr. President!

What?!!

Deputy: What?!
Me: What?!
Deputy: What?!
Me: What? No! No! Sorry, sir! I'm just thinking about our great president.
Deputy: What about our great president?

Salem… I hate you…

Me: Well… About… How… What really… A great… mission our president is taking on.
Deputy: What mission?

-Ok, Salem… To be honest, you deserve it.
-I do, I do… Crucify me!
-They will!

Me: Well... It's totally obvious... The mission of... Carrying this great nation... To a greater...

Deputy: Greater?

Me: Greater...

Deputy: ...Aha?

Me: Greater... position in this evil world. We wouldn't be able to take a single step forward without a farsighted great leader like that strong, intelligent, humanitarian, environmental, peace-seeking, firefighter, great leader.

- Firefighter?
- You said "great leader" twice!
- He won't notice! Now shut up!
- What the fuck is a firefighting president?

Deputy: Firefighter?

- Toldja!
- SHUT UP!

Me: It's a leader who protects his country. It's not an easy job sir!

Deputy: Aha... How does he do that?

Me: Right? It's an enormous amount of work.

Deputy: No, no, I am asking you, How does he do that?

Me: Oh... Well, I can't imagine how. My small mind can't comprehend it...

Deputy: Explain it!

Me:... I... it's... Umm...

The interrogation went on for 7 hours of questions and lectures on patriotism. Eventually, they let me go. I went home counting this as additional experience that'll be useful the next time they call me in.

Part III. Big Black Boots (2009)
Political Security Directorate

It's 8 am in the morning.

knock knock

Salem!

*knock knock knock *

Salem! Wake up!

Me: What is it, Mom? I Just slept.
Mom: Wake up!

I open the door.

Mom: There are two agents asking about you at the door.
Me: Tell them to come later... Wait WHAT?

I jump from the bed like an arrow.

Me: What agents?! Which department?!
Mom: I don't know. What did you do?
Me: I don't know! What did I do?
Mom: I don't know, Salem! It's probably about your hair again! I told you many times to shorten it!
Me: Let me deal with this, Mom. I'm not going to cut it!
Mom: Stop arguing now. Check those people.
Me: I'm not gonna shorten it.
Mom: Salem!
Me: Ok! Ok!

I go out to check them...

Mom: You're in your pyjamas!

Me: They are just damn agents.

I open the door and there they are. Two morons in uniforms. But don't get me wrong, not military or police uniforms. They are just two civilian-looking idiots, wearing what we started to call "uniforms" due to their all-too-obvious look. These people are supposed to act as if they don't want to be conspicuous because they are "undercover agents", yet they do everything possible to show their authority and to make every creature on earth know that they are "undercover agents". Not to mention their invariably greasy hair.

Me: Yes?

Agent 1: Are you...*checking papers* Zymolust S. Ravenson?

Me: Ugh... I am.

Agent 1: We need to talk to you.

Me: Okay?

Agent 1: So can we talk?

Me: Go ahead.

Agent 1: Can we come inside?

Me: Yea. Give me a second.

I hate my life!

Me: Come in.

They sit freely and make themselves at home.

Me: Make yourselves at home...

My Mom brings some coffee and sits with us.

Me: *whispering* Would you leave us alone, please?

Mom: No!

Me: *whispering* Why did you bring coffee?!

I'm sleepy and worried. I also hate them.

Me: How can I help you guys?

Agent 1: We want to ask you a couple of questions.

Me: Go ahead.

Please!

Agent 1: We want you tomorrow at the Political Security Directorate HQ.

POLITICAL SECURITY DIRECTORATE

Political Security Directorate (PSD) is an intelligence service of the Syrian government affiliated with the Ministry of Interior. The PSD was founded in 1963, and it is headquartered in Damascus, Syria. It is headed by a general who is appointed by the President of Syria. It monitors literature, print publications, political dissent and all media outlets.

What kind of question is that?

Me: Why?

Mom: Why?

Me: Mom!

Mom: He didn't do anything.

Me: Mom!

Mom: Is it because of his hair?

Me: What? Mom!

Agent 1: His what?

Me: Never mind.

Mom: It's just a style.

Agent 1: Why are you so afraid?

Me: No she is fine, she just wants to...

Mom: You know how things are when you people ask for someone.

Me: Mom!

Agent 1: Us people?

Me: Mom!

Mom: You know, you take people and...

Me: Mom! Mom! Mom! Thank you for the coffee, would you please leave us alone?

We have things to discuss. Thank You, Mom! Thank you!

Agent 2: What did she mean by "you take people"?

Me: She Meant nothing.

Agent 1: What?

Me: Never mind. Why am I wanted there?

Agent 1: You are not wanted, yet.

Agent 2: What does your mom mean, we take people?

Me: She means nothing, she is an old woman, you know.

Agent 1: She doesn't look old.

Me: Excuse me?!

Agent 2: She thinks we take people?

Me: No, no, no she just...

Agent 1: We're just gonna ask some questions.

Me: But I..

Agent 2: Does she think we take people just like that?

Me: No!

Agent 2: So what did she mean?

Agent 1: We have no idea why they want you there.

Me: They? So you guys are not from the Political Security Directorate?

Agent 2: By the way we don't take people for no reason.

Me: I know that.

Agent 1: We are from Political Security Directory but we can't give any more
information.

Agent 2: We only take the bad ones...

Me: So why are you taking me?

Agent 1: We're not taking you.

Agent 2: ...Those who are against this great country.

Me: I understand...?

Agent 1: As I told you, you're not wanted. We want to have a small chat with
you.

Me: So have it here.

Agent 2: She mentioned something about your hair.

Agent 1: We can't have a chat here.

Me: There is nothing about my hair.

Agent 1: What hair?

Me: *pointing at Agent 2* No no, I'm just talking to that guy.

Agent 2: What guy?

Agent 1: Tell us about that "guy".

Me: What guy?

Agent 2: You mentioned some guy.

Me: No, I was just talking to you!

Agent 2: I know, but I'm asking about the guy you're talking about.

Agent 1: (to Agent 2) What guy?

Agent 2: (to Agent 1) I don't know. I'm asking him.

OMG!

Me: Ok, guys! I'll be there first thing in the morning. Thank you for your visit. It's been a pleasure! *closing the door*

Me: Mom, I need some coffee...

The next day I'm standing at the gates of the Political Security Directory headquarters.

The political atmosphere in this country has been getting more strict since 2000, the year Bashar Assad inherited a farm called Syria from his dead father Hafiz. The whole thing started to get worse since my first arrest following the assassination of the Lebanese prime minister Rafiq Al-Hariri in 2005.

2006 HEZBOLLAH-ISRAEL WAR

The 2006 Lebanon War, also known as the July War or the Second Lebanon War, was a 34-day military conflict between Israel and Hezbollah. The conflict began on July 12, 2006, when Hezbollah launched a cross-border raid into Israel, killing three Israeli soldiers and capturing two others. Israel responded with a massive air and ground offensive, targeting Hezbollah strongholds in Lebanon and killing hundreds of civilians.

It went further downhill after the "fake war" between Hezbollah and Israel in 2006... These are wars in which Arab dictators collude with their enemies and strengthen their own despotic regimes whether they win or lose. There are countless examples of these fake wars.

The war of 1948 of more than five Arab armies against so-called Israel. All of

THE NAKBA

The Nakba (Arabic: النكبة, al-Nakbah, "the catastrophe") is the term used by Palestinians to describe the events of 1948, when over 700,000 Palestinians were displaced from their homes and became refugees. The Nakba is considered to be one of the most defining events in Palestinian history, and it continues to be a source of pain and trauma for many Palestinians.

The Nakba was the result of a combination of factors, including the 1948 Arab-Israeli War, the actions of the Israeli military, and the policies of the Israeli government. In the course of the war, the Israeli military expelled or displaced hundreds of thousands of Palestinians from their homes. The Israeli government also confiscated Palestinian land and property.

In the 1973 war, Syria and Egypt launched a coordinated attack against Israel to recapture the territory they had lost in the last war. In the end, neither side achieved their goals. In spite of thousands of Arab civilians who were killed by Israeli air strikes, Hafiz Assad and Anwar Sadat solidified their dictatorship in Syria and Egypt by declaring themselves heroes of the Arab world. To add insult to injury, Sadat became the first Arab leader to recognise Israel.

these armies were defeated in a few weeks largely due to their petty rivalries. This preventable disaster reduced the Arab resistance battalions that were marching to free Palestine. Arab regimes also wanted to ease the anger of Arab nations against the new cancer called Israel, as if to say: "Well we went to war but we lost... too bad, move on".

Next is the 1956 Suez Crisis. It was a small attack by France, UK and Israel against Egypt, which worked out as a propaganda boost for Abdul Nasser's dictatorship.

The 1967 war between Israel and Egypt was totally absurd. The Egyptian side kept blasting propaganda on the radio announcing victory. The announcements went as far as reassuring the public that the Egyptian army was at the gates of Jerusalem. But of course, it was a big fat lie. It shocked Arabs, from the Gulf to the Atlantic.

SUEZ CRISIS

The Suez Crisis was a military conflict that took place in October 1956, when Israel, France, and the United Kingdom invaded Egypt in response to Egypt's nationalization of the Suez Canal. The crisis was a major turning point in the Cold War, and it led to the withdrawal of all three countries from the canal.

The crisis began on July 26, 1956, when Egyptian President Gamal Abdel Nasser announced the nationalization of the Suez Canal. The canal was owned by a French-British company, and the nationalization was seen as a threat to Western interests in the region.

Guard: Hey! What do you want?

Me: I'm supposed to meet someone.

Guard: What?!

Me: I'm wanted.

Guard: Wanted by who?

Me: By you.

Guard: Name and phone!

I'm now sitting in a room waiting for the interrogator. After waiting for about 3 hours, some idiot finally enters the room. He sits at a desk with some papers and starts writing.

He: Your name.

Me: Zymolust S. Ravenson.

He: Your uncles live in Australia.

Me: My uncles? yes?

He: All of them?

Me: Most of them.

He: What are their political views?

Me: What political views?

He: Any political view.

Me: I don't understand.

He: What party do they belong to?

Me: I don't know, they have been in Australia for about 30 years.

He: they never visited you?

Me: They did.

He: So?

Me: So?

He: They never told you?

Me: Told me what?

He: Stop evading! Answer!

Me: I never asked them what their political views are.

He: Mmm

silence

The Six-Day War was a war fought between Israel and a coalition of Arab states from June 5 to 10, 1967. The war began when Israel launched a surprise attack on Egypt, Syria, and Jordan. Israel quickly defeated the Arab armies and captured the Sinai Peninsula, the Golan Heights, the West Bank, and East Jerusalem.

The Six-Day War was a major turning point in the Arab-Israeli conflict. It led to a significant shift in the balance of power in the region, and it made Israel the dominant military power in the Middle East. The war also had a profound impact on the Palestinian people, who were displaced from their homes in the West Bank and Gaza Strip.

He: So you've been to Egypt a few months ago.

Me: Yes.

He: What were you doing there?

Me: College.

He: Studying?

Gosh...

Me: Yes.

He: What were your studies about?

Me: It's Commercial Diving.

He: Aha, business administration.

Me: No, it's...

He: Banking?

Me: No, no, it's like...

He: So it's something like accounting.

Me: It's surface supply diving.

He: Surface? So you dive but like on land? How come?

Me: No, The air we use is on the surface, on land.

He: You mean the oxygen?

Me: It's just normal compressed air.

He: Yes I understand, oxygen.

Just say yes, man!

Me: Yes, it's oxygen.

He: So it's not real diving.

Me: No it's not.

He: Why did you go then?

Omg...

Me: I went for pleasure

He: So you just went there to have fun?

Me: Yes.

He: So you meant "swimming" by "diving"

Me: Yes

He: Be specific next time!

Me: Yes, sir.

He: Ok, so two years ago you were interrogated by the Military Security in-
telligence
Me: Yes.
He: Why?

Here we go.

Me: I was accused of being a Satanist.
He: Aha, So you're a Satanist.
Me: No! Just accused of it.
He: So you're not a Satanist.
Me: No.
He: How can we be sure?
Me: They let me go.
He: So why do you grow your hair?

I'm not gonna cut it!!

Me: It's a style.
He: Are you homosexual?!
Me: No! No! It's just a style.
He: So you look better with long hair?
Me: I don't know. I think so.
He: Do you want to tell me that you grow your hair for no reason?

SON OF A BITCH!

Me: It's nothing more than a style. That is the reason. Style!
He: Then what about your boots?
Me: What about them?
He: You tell me.
Me: Tell you what?
He: About your boots.
Me: What about them?
He: I'm asking you!
Me: I don't understand the question.
He: I want to know about these boots!
Me: Well, these are nice boots and...
He: No! That's not my question.

Me: You're asking about my boots

He: Yes!

Me: I'm answering.

He: No! I want to know why you wear
these kinds of boots?

Processing...

Me: What boots?

He: These kinds of boots! Big black boots!

-What? I think I'm hearing him
wrong. Maybe I should rewind my
brain and listen again.
! So back *Rewind memory, press
play*:

     "I want to know why you wear
these kinds of boots?
     Big black boots!"

-Look, man, you better make sure.
Because I don't think this is a
thing.

Me: You want to know why I wear these kinds of boots, right?

He: Yes!

-So it's real, man. It's a real
question.
-Now answer the moron. Why do you
wear these kinds of boots?
-But not any kind of boots! Big
black boots!

Me: I also have sneakers.

He: But why do you wear these kinds of boots?

Me: Big black boots?

He: Exactly.

Me: I don't always wear these.

He: You're wearing them right now.

So this is the latest crime nowa-
days?

I look down at my feet with voices rag-
ing in my head:

-Great choice, man.
-What did you want me to say in-
stead?
-Ha? You only have big black boots!
-I also have brown ones.
-Shut up! Answer the idiot!

Me: Well...

Well what? Well what?

He: Well what?

-I don't know what to say...
-Great!
-It's a stupid question!
-No kidding!
-What will you say, smart ass?
-I don't know! Help me out here.
-We are the same person, fool! An-
swer!

Me: Well,

He: Well?

Me: It's probably for two reasons.

He: Probably?

I need to come up with something.
I need to come up with something
now!

He: Are you trying to come up with something?

Me: No. I'm not trying to come up with something!

He: So what are the two reasons?

Me: First reason is because of school.

He: School? What school?

Me: Our schools. You made us wear these kinds of "boots" along with a military

uniform back in the day. It was mandatory to do so. We couldn't enter school
otherwise. That's how I got used to them.

Good job, man!

He: And the second reason?

Did you really have to say "two reasons"?

Me: What second reason?
He: You said two reasons, what is the second one?

Me: The second reason is...

drumming in my head

-What the fuck, man?
-J'm bored!
-Just come up with something!

Me: It's because of the streets.
He: Streets?
Me: Yes, the streets are very very bad, I can't walk without hurting my feet
if I don't wear these kinds of boots.

- Phew!
- Good answer.
- Right?
- Yes.
- Hi five!
- Shut up!

He: Aha. *writing* Ok. So, do you ever
light fires on your balcony?
Me: You mean for a BBQ.
He: No! I said fire! Fire!
Me: I don't smoke shisha.
He: I said fire! Do you not understand?

There is only one kind of fire left, man...

BLACKENED EARTH BEFORE ME
-Hey!

CREEPING FOG IN MY WAY
-Hello!

LURKING THROUGH THE SHADOWS OF ANOTHER DAY
-OMS...

MY HEART'S THE DARKENED ONE, MY SOUL ON ICE
-Stop!

INTO THE WORLD BENEATH ME

I STALK THE NIGHHHHT

-Gosh! Salem! Stop playing this track! Say something!

Me: Do you mean a fire like "fire"?
He: Yes.
Me: As in flames?
He: Yes.

I'm not convinced. Let's give him an example just to make sure he is not sane.

Me: You mean as in, do I ever get some gasoline, pour it all over my balcony then light it up?
He: Yes! Don't you understand "fire"?

Ok, he is insane.

Me: Umm...Nope... I'm not in the habit of doing that.
He: I see. What about blood?
Me: I don't drink blood either.
He: I didn't say anything about drinking. I mean do you conduct any rituals

with blood?

Me: Rituals? No!

He: Something like...

Me: I don't do rituals.

He: ...like covering your body with blood?

I also ride black unicorns... WTF is this?!

He: Cat's blood to be precise.

Me: What? No! No way. I'm a Mus...

-Don't! Don't say it!
Don't open another hell upon you!
You're about to be a terrorist.

Me: I don't... I swear.

He: But we have a report.

Me: They are lying.

He: I didn't tell you what it says.

Me: Whatever it's saying, it's a lie.

He: You're saying that we lie in our reports.

Get out of this now.

Me: I'm saying that I don't do any rituals. Do you think my family would allow such a thing?

He: Maybe they don't know.

This is our chance!

Me: I know for sure, sir, that you deal with facts. Great responsibilities like yours can not be achieved with "maybes".

He: The report says that you have skulls in your bedroom.

Me: I don't have skulls in my bedroom.

He: How do we know?

SEARCH MY GODDAMN ROOM!

Me: Search my... room.

He: Maybe you'll hide them.

Me: I'm not gonna hide them.

He: So you do have skulls.

Me: I don't have skulls.

He: If you had skulls, what would you use them for?

Me: Exactly, I have no idea what a person uses a skull for.

He: Medical schools use them, for example.

Me: Never even passed by a medical school.

He: Or maybe to cast some spells?

I wanna cast a boot over you!

Me: I don't know.

A new man walks into to room and calls out to the interrogator:

The Man: Moheeb! Talk to the captain!

Moheeb: Right away.

Thank God! What a torture!

About an hour later Moheeb came back and told me to leave.

Me: What about my ID?

Moheeb: We will call you.

Me: Can I have some receipt that says you have my ID?

Moheeb: What receipt? It's not a supermarket. We will call you!

I leave the building thinking about the reason for all that. It's totally use-less. What a waste of resources, time and breath.

Me: Hi Mom.

Mom: What happened? What did they want you for?

Me: My boots...

Mom: Boots? What boots?

Me: Never mind, you won't believe it anyway.

A Week Later

phone ringing

Me: Yes?

Someone: We want you to come right now.

Me: What? Who is this?

Moheeb: It's me, Moheeb. You don't recognize my voice?

Jumping from a building would hurt a lot, that's why I don't do it.

Me: Oh, yes. Of course, I recognize your voice.

He: Come now if you want to have your ID.

Me: Ok I'll be there ASAP.

He: But don't be in those black boots! The Captain wants to check you before releasing your ID.

Me: Oh, of course. *hangs up*

My brother had silver-coloured sneakers. Yes, silver. Way too silver. So I put them on and went there.

Guard: What are you?

Me: I am here for...

Guard: Name and phone.

I entered, met Moheeb inside and he made sure that I was not wearing those boots. His smile was big and it was so obvious that he was so satisfied I'm wearing the dumbest shoes ever.

He took me to the captain's room.

knock knock

Captain: Enter.

Moheeb: *opens the door* All respects sir!

Captain: What is it?

Moheeb: The Criminal Zymolust S. Ravenson

-Criminal?
-Yea, at least you're not a terrorist
this time.
-I think it's cool to be a criminal
in Syria.
-Really!?
-Of course!
-It's a pair of goddamn BLACK
BOOTS!! For fuck sake!!
-It's Syria!
-It's hell!
-What's the difference?

Captain: Are you Z. S. R?

Me: Z. S. R.? Yes I am Z. S. R.

Moheeb: He is a good boy now Sir. He is dressed the right way now.

I also grew a tail!

Captain: What about the hair?

Moheeb: He promised he will shorten it sir.

Me: Yes? Umm, I will trim that... Thing... Sir.

Captain: You see, if you ever wanna get married you will never be accepted by
any family. Do you understand this?

Accepted? What the hell is this moron talking about?

Me: Yes, sir.

Captain: So our advice to you is to dress like normal people.

How about socks?

Me: Yes, sir.

Captain: I don't want to see you here again!

Me: Yes, sir.

Captain: Get him out!

Me: But sir, about my ID?

Captain: Yea, yea. Give him his ID back, Moheeb.

Moheeb: Yes, sir!

Got my ID and went back home.

Mom: What happened?

Me: Nothing.

Mom: No, tell me. Did they do anything to you?

Me: No, I'm fine.

Mom: They didn't say anything?

Me: They like my shoes...

Mom: What?

Me: I know...

Mom: I don't understand.

Me: Me neither.

Mom: Coffee?

Me: Coffee...

Part IV. Spyfully Yours. (2011)

Political Security Directorate

It's early 2011, my friend and his guest enter the little local cafe in Tartous where we usually meet. His guest is a foreigner, which is common since he works at a hotel in Damascus and meets many people from different countries. He introduces us to each other and we sit in that cafe for a couple of hours. Two days later, I am watching the news. These are the early days of the revolution and following the news has become a daily habit in my routine.

FLASH NEWS! SPY CAUGHT IN SYRIA

The headlines flash on Syrian National TV. The official state channel that broadcasts bullshit 24/7. And there I see my friend's guest sitting right there confessing to working for Israel! The photos he had taken are shown on TV as evidence that he is some kind of spy. But all I can see are a bunch of goddamn trees that happen to be Syrian and some other crap of no use for espionage. "100 Egyptian Pounds per photo," he says. I'm shocked, I'm afraid, I'm gone... And I'm wondering:

Why did they make him say Egyptian pounds instead of US dollars? It would have made more sense! They can't even tell a proper lie!

While the implausibility of their lie simmers in my mind another fear comes to a boil:

They will be after me in no time!

Imagine being a Lebanese national in Syria. Now imagine seeing the guy you sat together in a café, announcing on national TV that he is a spy for Israel. Right at the beginning of a revolution that the regime calls an "Israeli conspiracy." Now check your pulse!

I don't know what to do. I can't call my friend who introduced me to the "spy"! It would be dangerous for us to communicate! I decide to stay home for a few days, just until the story is forgotten. Or maybe for a brand new equally bullshit headline to appear on national TV to wipe out this story.

A week goes by, and everything seems to be kinda normal. I leave home and take a walk in the neighborhood. Nothing suspicious. I decide to go to that little cafe for a cup of coffee and to sniff around. I enter the cafe acting normally and see the owner approach me. He usually asks what I would like to drink.

Me: Hey, bro. Get me the usual.

Owner: Two agents from The Political Intelligence are asking about you.

Me: Excuse me?!

Owner: Two agents from Political...

Me: I got it! I got it! What did they ask you about?

Owner: They are right here, next to the cafe. They are asking about you now! I mean right now!

Me: Now!

Owner: Right N...

Me: I got it! I got it!

Owner: They've been asking about you for about a week. It's a matter of national security, they say.

Me: National security?

Owner: They are out there. You should go talk to them now. It won't take more than a few minutes.

Me: Keep those minutes to yourself! You fuckn' rat!

That owner is so excited about getting me detained by those criminals. I walk out to meet three guys, not two, one of them is a skinny, grey-haired bastard.

Sergeant Ali: Are you Zymolust S. Ravenson?!

Me: *pause* I am... Unfortunately.

Sergeant Ali: We would like to have a very small conversation with you. It won't take more than a few minutes. Do you prefer it here or at the Department?

Me: Well, yea, regarding those minutes—

Sergeant Ali: I think it's better that we go to the department. What do you think?

Me: Well...

Two of them grab my arms and put me in that terri-fying white Peugeot 505 station wagon. The car that terrorized generations of Syri-ans across the country. Throughout the ride, I try to think about what to say during the interrogation. I can't deny that I met the "spy". I can say that there could have been many "rats" in that cafe, and in any other cafe or a public place in Syria for that matter. What should I say? If I say I never met him, they would get even more suspicious about me. Because they seem to have evidence I met him. If I say Yes I met him, they will consider this to be a confession and things

will be
even
worse!
I also
can't
act
stupid
and
be a
to-

SAYDNAYA AND TADMOR PRISONS

Saydnaya Military Prison and Tadmor Prison are two of the most notorious prisons in Syria. They are both located in the Homs governorate, and they have been used to detain political prisoners and dissidents for decades.

The United Nations Commission of Inquiry on Syria (COI) has documented cases of torture, arbitrary detention, and extrajudicial killings at both prisons. The COI has also found that the Syrian government has failed to provide adequate food, water, and sanitation to prisoners at Sednaya and Tadmor prisons. As a

In 2015, the COI estimated that between 5,000 and 13,000 people had been killed in Sednaya prison since 2011. However, the COI has since stated that this number is likely to be an underestimate.

tal moron for long. Not this time, it won't work. My brain is trying itself as we get closer to the department of one-way ticket to Saydnaya or Tadmor. Now we are there, I'm sitting in a dark room with a single light bulb, just like some cheap B-movie.

Sergeant Ali: So, are we going to talk or not?

Me: Sorry sir, I don't und–

Sergeant Ali: You are here for a matter of national security. Denying and holding information won't be good for you.

Me: Of Course, sir, I...

Sergeant Ali: Don't Try to deny anything! We know everything!

Me: I totally–

Sergeant Ali: So you heard about the spy we caught in Damascus?

Me: A spy? In Damascus? Where?

Sergeant Ali: In Damascus! You just said it yourself, in Damascus!

Me: Yes I understand, sir, but I never heard about that. I'm totally shocked.

Sergeant Ali: Shocked?

Me: Surprised.

Sergeant Ali: Surprised?

Fucked!

Me: I'm just worried about this great nation. This is dangerous, sir.

Sergeant Ali: Tell us then, what were you doing with him in that cafe about ten days ago?

Me: Him? Him who?

Sergeant Ali: So you want us to try different measures to make you talk?

Me: I'm sorry, sir, but I'm trying to understand.

Sergeant Ali: You were sitting with that spy ten days ago. Will you tell us now what you were planning?

We were planning for a coup! Fuckin' moron!

Me: Planning? Sir, I'm sure there is a huge misunderstanding. I'm trying to remember because I want to help. Would you please give me more details about that criminal?

Sergeant Ali: He is Egyptian, do you remember a guy with an Egyptian accent? You don't see Egyptians every day in Tartous, right?

Me: Right. Actually one of my friends had a guest with him, but to be honest, I'm not sure if he's Egyptian or Iraqi, maybe he was Algerian, Moroccan, Sudanese or something like that. I'm not sure anymore.

Sergeant Ali: These are totally different accents! How in the hell can you confuse these accents? Besides! He is not black enough to be Sudanese!

Me: I don't know any other accent but ours. I remember now that there was a foreigner. That's right. Besides, Sudanese can be as white as...

Sergeant Ali: Now tell me! What did you talk about? What things do you plot against the regime?

Me: God forbid! I can't betray this country. The country that fed me, educated me, gave me everything that a mother would give to her child, a sister would give to her brother, a husband would give to his...

Sergeant Ali: Answer the question! What did you talk about?

Me: Well I think it was all about gaming and stuff.

Sergeant Ali: Gaming? Are you kidding me!!

Me: No no sir, I mean—

Sergeant Ali: Answer the goddamn question.

Me: I am, sir, I am. The guy is fascinated with mobile games. I just remembered that he said something about "Super Mario".

Sergeant Ali: Super Mario? That's a football player. Is that what you meant by gaming?

Me: Umm, yes sir, he is kinda into football...as well... if you say so.

Sergeant Ali: *writing on a paper with a look of fulfilment* What is his favourite team?

Me: Well, since his favourite player's name is "Mario", I guess he is supporting Italy.

Sergeant Ali: What about your friend?

Me: He also supports Italy..

Sergeant Ali: What the hell are you talking about?

Me: I know, sir. Not such an amazing team.

Sergeant Ali: I'm asking you about your friend! You idiot!

Me: Which one?

Sergeant Ali: Don't act stupid! The one who was with him.

Me: Oh yes. He didn't say much. He was busy with his phone.

Sergeant Ali: Talking to who? Was he communicating with someone abroad?

Me: No, no sir I don't think so, I think he was talking with his girlfriend.

He: Fine. Listen, I'll let you go home now, but, tomorrow morning, you will come here, call that friend, put him on speaker, and act normal while you ask about that spy, what he knows about him and other questions. I'll write to you so you can memorize them. Do you understand?

- Say yes!
- You traitor! What about your friend?
- We will figure something out!!! Yes! Yes! Say yes!

Me: Absolutely sir. Anything for this great country.

I go back home after only a few hours! It's a miracle! I send a coded email to my friend, explaining everything. I advise him to acknowledge knowing the "spy" and nothing more. The next day I'm in the department with Sgt. Ali. My friend and I perform exactly as we rehearsed. We were supposed to be done with that since Sgt. Ali has no more suspicions about me anymore.

But there's one last thing...

Sergeant Ali: We are done now. We are keeping your ID.

Me: My ID? But why sir? Am I not done yet?

Sergeant Ali: You are. We just have to keep it for a while, for security reasons.

Me: But sir, no one can walk without an ID in Syria.

Sergeant Ali: Syria?

Me: I mean... umm... this country.

Sergeant Ali: This country?

Me: Our Country?

Sergeant Ali: What Country?

Me: Syria.

Sergeant Ali: Syria?

Me: I mean, sir, I can't walk the streets without an ID. What if someone from one of those intelligence departments stopped me, or I was taken by them? How can I prove it is me?

Sergeant Ali: Are you afraid of something you committed?

Me: No, no absolutely not sir. It is just a matter of being lawful.

Sergeant Ali: Then tell them that your ID is in the Department.

Me: What Department?

Sergeant Ali: This Department! Are you stupid?

Me: I mean, can I have a receipt or som-

Sergeant Ali: A receipt? That is total nonsense! You think you're at the movies? Tell them your ID is with Sergeant Ali.

Of course! That hadn't occurred to me!

Me: But sir I just want...

Sergeant Ali: Come back in three days and take your damn ID! You don't have to walk the streets during these 3 days, stay home. Leave now before I change my mind.

Me: Yes sir!

3 days later, I'm at the gates of the Political Intelligence Directorate. They take my phone and escort me to a room. It's kinda small, there are about ten people inside. I sit on the floor. Waiting for Sgt. Ali, so I can get my ID back as promised. I wait and wait and then wait a little more but he doesn't show up. Around 8 pm they tell me to get back tomorrow. Sgt. Ali is on a mission...

I come back the next day. Sit in the room and wait. 8pm: Sgt. Ali is on a mission. Get back tomorrow.

The day after: room, wait, mission, Tomorrow.

For 26 glorious days, home to the department, department to home. I become
a regular "customer" at the department.
One of the guards almost about to smiles
at my face once! Some of my friends
and even relatives start to think I'm
working for them!

After about a month, Sgt. Ali arrives at
last.

I can't believe it, I almost cry with
happiness! I finally have my ID in my
hands!
One of my friends calls to congratulate
me. I call my dad to deliver the good
news, he congratulates me... Then tells me
that two agents from the "General Intelligence Directorate" are waiting for me at
our house. They need to ask me a couple
of questions at the Department of General Intelligence Directorate! I go back home
to face another phase of horror, this time
its the General Intelligence Directorate! The
name itself makes any sane person piss
their pants. But thank God I haven't
got an ounce of sanity in me. A sane
person wouldn't stay a minute in this
country.

I arrive home and meet those two agents.
Walking towards them as if I'm totally
normal was one of the bravest things I
did in my life.

Agent 1: Are you Zymolust S. Ravenson?

- Say "YES" with glory!
- Shut up!

Me: I am, but I wish I was my cousin!

I'm in handcuffs this time, led by them to the goddamn white Peugeot! We are now going to one of Syria's deepest abysses: The Katar Sousa State Security Building!

Part V. Into the Abyss (2011)
Department of State Security Intelligence

It's the end of May

The car smells like mouldy old fabric that's been marinating in the methane of a hundred cops' asses. The steering wheel is wrapped in a spongy cover. It probably used to be beige, but now it's just gross with filthy hand marks all over.

I Must focus... It must be about the "spy" case again. Or maybe it has something to do with "satanism". But really it could be any number of accusations drawn from the Assad family bingo.

Sitting in the back seat of that car between two "unintelligent" intelligence agents is not an easy ride in Syria. The feeling is as bad as sitting before the interrogator of the General Intelligence Directorate. The interrogation starts with a short lecture, then proceeds with questions and threats.

GENERAL INTELLIGENCE DIRECTORATE

The General Intelligence Directorate (GID) is the main intelligence agency of Syria. It is responsible for gathering intelligence on both domestic and foreign threats to the Syrian government. The GID is also responsible for conducting covert operations and for suppressing dissent. The GID was founded in 1946, shortly after Syria gained independence from France. The agency was originally known as the Political Security Directorate, but it was renamed the General Intelligence Directorate in 1969.

Interrogator: This is a strong state... What's going on these days is nothing but a global conspiracy against Syria. Taking part in this conspiracy leads to one's grave.

Me: Agreed.

He: Don't speak unless I order you to, understood?

Me: ...

He: Good. Now, confess. Tell me everything you know about these terrorists. How and when do you communicate? Tell us about the weapons, your intentions, and above all, who is financing you.

Me: *sweating*

He: speak!

Me: I... no.

He: no what?

Me: I have no clue at all. Not a single vague idea in a dream about what you, sir, are talking about.

He: I'm talking about smuggling weapons to terrorists.

Me: The only weapon I know is my mother's kitchen knife. I don't know anything about anything else.

He: We have evidence against you. Official reports from the central General Intelligence Directory in Damascus. So it is easier for you to confess.

Me: I don't know what these weapons are about.

Interrogator: *Calls out to someone* Take this thing meaning me to room nine, he needs time to remember.

And as a thing, I am taken to a room with some wooden chairs. I sit there waiting. It takes him about two or three hours to call me back. Meanwhile, in that room, I am not allowed to walk, stand, or even wriggle in my seat. The only thing I am allowed to do is to breathe and blink. It's an unwritten rule everyone born in Syria knows. So walking back to the interrogator feels pretty good, believe it or not.

Interrogator: Did you decide to confess?

Me: I'm not sure what to confess sir.

He: Smuggling weapons for terrorists in Syria, financed by The Future Movement of Lebanon.

-Of course...
-Just kill me...
-You wish!
-I'm wishing
for it, moron!!
-Yea, yea. Answer the
damn cock sucker...

THE FUTURE MOVEMENT

The Future Movement.(Arabic: تيار المستقبل, Tayyar al-Mustaqbal) is a political party in Lebanon. It is the largest Sunni Muslim party in Lebanon. The Future Movement was founded in 1995 by Rafik Hariri, who was then the Prime Minister of Lebanon. The party's founding was a response to the Syrian occupation of Lebanon.

تيار المستقبل

Me: Oh, The Future... Movement? I have no relations or connections in Lebanon. Especially with regard to politics.

He: I have reports!

Me: I have no doubt... that you do, sir, but I'm not the person you're looking for. I fear that I might be wasting your precious time.

He: The report says you are in contact with a female in Homs to send her weapons.

Me: I know no "female" in Homs.

He: Maybe you know a guy that you're dealing with?

Me: The only thing I know about Homs is The Bakery of Homs two streets from my house. Right here in Tartous.

So, he sends me back to the same room
again for a few more hours.

Later, he personally comes into the room
to ask me the following question, believe
it or not:

He: What is your favourite type of dolma? Cabbage leaves, courgettes or vine leaves with mutton?

What? What kind of questions is
this? Must be a trick question! I
mean any sane person would pick
vine leaves. Especially if they are
cooked with some ribs.

Me: I like them all, sir.

He: Choose.

Me: Maybe I'll go for vine leaves.

He: Aha!

Damn! Are vine leaf dolmas too Sunni? I should have chosen cabbages instead.

He: I told you I have evidence! Check that.

He shows me part of the report which seems like a scanned conversation on some social media chat that reads: "My name is Salem and my favourite food is vine leaf dolmas."

Me:

silent

He: I can't overlook this hard evidence!

If you call this hard, I really feel sorry for your wife.

Me: silent
He: It's about time you confessed.
Me: It's a very weird piece of evidence.
He: Weird evidence?!
Me: Coincidence! Weird coincidence! Yet I believe from the depths of my heart that anyone, I mean anyone in this vast land would have chosen that meal, sir. It's dolma with vine leaves! With meat and ribs!
He: I didn't say ribs.
Me: Yes, sorry... But they're amazing when cooked with some ribs. It's not even necessary though. I would've chosen vine leaves even without ribs, to be honest.
He: So it is you!
Me: No no, sir, I'm saying that—
He: interrupting What about the name, Salem?
Me: There are millions of Salems in this world, sir.
He: Millions?
Me: Maybe a few dozen.

He: staring

Me: Okay. But I assure you, sir, I have nothing to do with this conversation. Anybody could've chosen vine leaf dolmas.

He: Listen, two hours till 5 pm. I must make a decision regarding your case. If you don't confess I will escalate your case to the capital. You know what they do in the capital. Be wise.

He's got nothing on me, he's bluffing. He is not sending me anywhere. Bullshit!

Next thing I know I am in handcuffs heading to the capital.

It's dark. I am thirsty. I have a metallic taste in my mouth. I read once that it's an indicator of brain disease/stroke. Although I am blindfolded, I can see from a certain angle. The handcuffs are too tight and I need to breathe.

-Calm down. You need to think.
-But thinking won't help this time. In fact, it never did.
-Ok then, at least prepare your mind for the hell that is approaching.
-It's taking too long...
-I want to get there ASAP. It it doesn't start it won't end.

I find myself in the reception room of the State Security Department receiving what is colloquially known as Hell's Reception. It starts with a punch to the face, followed by more punches and kicks, slaps, whip lashes and lots of hate. I don't even mention all the swearing. All of these are administered by a squad of professional torturers standing in line on both sides, taking turns.

This introduction goes on for about five
minutes, until I am dragged to the reception room.
I am there on my knees receiving kicks
from two animals while some thugs check
my pockets for valuables to steal.

One of them finds my ID and asks: "Is this your ID, Lebanese bitch?"

I have a burning desire to tell him:
"No, it's my favourite mug, you damn
idiot! Of course, it's my cursed ID!"

Me: Yes, Si..

A kick prevents me from saying more.
Just minutes later, I am half fall-
ing down the stairs toward the basement
cells. As a kid, I had always heard stories that detainees were told by their torturers:

"God does not exist here!"

I am taken into a cell, which was made
to be the jailors' "office". They are all
hanging out there, on an iron bed frame
having Sheesha.

Jailer: What's your name, you animal?

Me: My name is...

SLAP

Jailer: Shut the fuck up! What is your name?

Me: silent

Jailer: Answer me, you animal!

SLAP

Me: My Name...

SLAP

Jailer: Take him to the hole!

I am
a 90 kg man, dragged
from my long straight black
hair. I would not recommend it
to anyone, but it's actually physical-
ly possible. This idea flashes through my
mind while half my hair is being torn off
my head...

Then I am in The Hole.

The Hole is a disgusting room with faucets installed
on white ceramic tiles and buckets of cold water on
the floor. I stop feeling anything after the fourth
or fifth lash of the whip. I guess it's a mechanism
the brain uses to reduce pain and humiliation.
I'm naked, it's freezing. The floor is disgusting
with dust, dry blood and stains that look
like grease. But I'm trying to embrace it,
as a futile attempt to remain invul-
nerable to the whip that corrodes
a part of my soul with every
hit.

Here I am. Everything I heard about, everything I tried to avoid is right here. I am now a detainee. I am being tortured, like in those stories I heard throughout my meaningless life. I try to over-scream. The more I scream the more satisfied they become. This helps to keep the violence at a stable level. If you try to be some kinda superhero in these situations, the torturers will escalate the pain they inflict.

From the age of twelve, I had to wear a military uniform to school and receive training from military personnel, who beat us harder if we tried to hide our pain. Syrians of my generation were taught to appease our torturers from a very early age. You have to put on a performance of agony to entertain your captors. Otherwise you'll end up being a fool with no audience, hence no show. They want to watch you suffer, so just be a sport and indulge them.

I try to ignore the swearing. But these words hurt. Those filthy reptiles talk about my mother and my father in a very disgusting way. I'm so angry! I'm so afraid! I'm in so much pain!

Me: Oh God!

Torturer 1: Fuck your God. Where the fuck is your God?

Torturer 2: Oh he is calling for God! Hasan! Bring me "God"

Introducing "God", it's a quadruple cable made to be used as a whip. With one hit, I feel my legs jolt in a running motion. But I am going nowhere... Instead, I slip on the red puddle staining the white ceramic floor.

Torturer 1: Scream more you bastard!

Torturer 2: Look at his filthy blood! Disgusting!

Torturer 1: Is that enough?

Torturer 2: Let's end this with a "finishing".

The man weighing about 80 - 85 kg on my body with military boots is way more merciful than "God".

My wet hair -or what's left of it- is all over my face when they kick my head. It must be the cherry on their brutal cake. They use my body to wipe The Hole. handcuffed, blindfolded, thrown in a small cell, naked and wet.

-I am done.
-Breathe…
-It's real.

My clothes are next to me but I am not allowed to put them on. No Sleep. Every hour or so I get randomly tortured by a random torturer.

I know how dogs eat now. It was an order.

Won't mention the so-called "toilets".

Four or five days pass. They take off the handcuffs and the blindfold. I wish they hadn't. Seeing their faces is worse than I imagined. lights are on 24/7. I lose track of time. I don't know what day it is, nor what time.

They put me in a collective cell with clothes on. We are about 40 detainees, from Damascus, Homs, Albu Kamal, Idlib, Douma, Hama, Jarablus, Al Ghouta and of course myself, from Tartous.

It's not cool to be a "Sunni" from Tartous in one of Assad's abysses. But it's way worse to be the only long-haired detainee. Every time the jailer goes in he calls out: "Get me that long-haired male!"

Oh... Now I realize why the jailers decided not to shave my head!

The sound of a jailer kicking the cell's iron door shatters my incredibly rational thought. A new "herd" is being brought in. Shaved detainees wearing what once must have been white underwear. They are being kicked and thrown into the cell. Watching is harder than receiving. You might think, at least they are busy trying to kill someone else. But I assure you, you will not think so once you see other people being tortured.

Thin, fat, old, young, all kinds. There are doctors, butchers, students, pimps, electricians and small shop owners. That kid is 14... That man is 65. A guy with a bullet in his body is among them! I see colours on those half-naked men I can't believe human skin was capable of turning. Purple. But it is too purple! Is that make-up? Is it an illusion?

B r e a t h e...

Is it day or night? My brain can't tell. No brain can, not under these circumstances.
When we are allowed to sleep, we sleep on our sides facing each other's feet. We are about 50 now, in a medium cell.

We sleep with the lights on. White fluorescent lights.

I have time to think about those who

always said that Assad knows nothing
about this.
Systematic, purposely inflicted terror and
torture. My desire to laugh sarcastically
is broken by my effort to remember how
long I have been here.

You say 20 days, I say 25! Can't re-
mem-

a terrorizing kicking on the iron door

Jailer: WAKE UP ANIMALS!

We, "the animals", wake up terrorized as
usual. If you're not terrorized yet, you
better be before the jailer notices a glint
of defiance in your eyes. Stand up fast
and run to the corner, and you better
pray to God -not the whip- that you
wake up before anyone else, so you can
run to the corner before the jailer appears
at the door. Otherwise, he will have you
for breakfast.

Jailer 1: (to Jailer 2) Get me the long-haired mule!

- That's not fair! I'm closer to the
cor- oh! Ok. long-haired, again.
-Here you go super-hair. Just tell
me how many times your mom told
you to shorten it. Ha? Just tell me
how-

slap

Jailer: Where are you from you disgusting mule?

That's a good question.

Me: From Tartous, sir.
Jailer: Aha! Tartous.

I hope he doesn't ask about my-

He: What's your name?

... Would you please stop hoping?

Me: Zymolust S. Ravenson, sir.
Jailer: What does your ugly S. stand for? Don't tell me, it stands for "Ass"
Haha!

I don't know what I'm afraid to lose
first, my sanity or my sense of humour.

Me: It stands for Salem, sir.
Jailer: Fuck your name. And fuck that name.

slap

Jailer: Don't you agree?
Me: I agree sir.

punch

He: shut up you animal! Do you want freedom?

whip

Say no, say no, man.

Jailer: Say no!

slap

Me: No sir, no sir, I don't want freedom.

slap

Jailer: What do you want, pig? slap What do you want?

I don't know what I want, I never really did. Moving to Syria in the early 90s was not an easy thing for me. Pictures of Hafiz Assad -Bashar's Father- were literally in public bath- rooms. The dictator was everywhere. I heard my dad say once that he wouldn't be surprised if he opened the fridge one day and found a picture of Hafiz Assad.

Assad's schools are no different, they want to shove Assad's ideology down our throats. No Choice! One pres- ident, one party, one past, one future, one idea, no politics. They made sure that—

slap

HAFIZ ASSAD

Hafiz Assad was the president of Syria from 1971 to 2000. He was a member of the Ba'ath Party, and a key figure in the Syrian military.

In 1970, Assad led a coup d'état against the sitting president, Nureddin al-Atassi. Assad became president, and he ruled Syria for the next 30 years.

From a human rights perspective, Hafez al-Assad's presidency was a disaster. He was responsible for widespread human rights abuses, including arbitrary detention, torture, extrajudicial killings, disappearances, restrictions on freedom of expression, and discrimination against certain groups.

Jailer: What do you want?!

Say something man!

Me: I want Mr President Bashar Assad!

slap

Jailer: Say it again!
Me: I want Mr President Bashar Assad!

slap

Jailer: Again, mule!
Me: I don't want freedom! I want Mr. President Bashar Assad!
I don't want freedom! I want Mr. President Bashar Assad!
I don't want freedom! I want Mr. President Bashar Assad!

slap

You can only have one of them, indeed.

Blindfolded, handcuffed, led upstairs. I'm going to be interrogated at last. Wait a minute! What is this feeling? Oh! It's the sun! I can feel the sun! How beautiful! I can feel sunlight on my skin! Tears fill my eyes behind the blindfold, it's daytime! I must be passing through a courtyard. But of course, that's how they build torture facilities in Syria, a few buildings surrounding a courtyard. What a beautiful fee-

kick

Jailer: Get in, you animal!

On my knees.

Interrogator: to the jailer Why didn't you shave that animal?
Jailer: The head jailer ordered not to.
Interrogator: Fine, leave.

I hear a song on the radio, it's
coming from another room. It is nice
to-

Interrogator: Your name?!

Me: Zymolust S. Ravenson, sir.

Interrogator: Confess!

Me: I totally will.

Interrogator: Talk, Animal!

Me: I was talking to some "female" from Homs and she told me to protest but I
refused.

Interrogator: That's not what we want you to confess, bastard!

Me: Just tell me, sir. I am ready.

Interrogator: Your accusations are:

Interrogator: 1- Planning a coup against the regime.

Oh! This one is new.

Interrogator: 2- Helping and smuggling weapons to terrorists.

Yea, I heard that one before. Dealing
with the Future party of Lebanon,
you know, Lebanese, Lebanon, smuggling! It makes sense. I'd make up
the same accusation if I were them.

Interrogator: 3- Glorifying and reestablishing the "state of Ummayad".

Yea. Wait! What?! Ummayad?

Interrogator: 4- Planning and inciting genocide against the Alawites in the
Levant!

Genocide? Levant?... Ummayad?

Interrogator: 5- Taking part in a global conspiracy against Syria and the
President of Syria Dr Bashar al Assad!

Global... No one heard of him before
2012.

Me: I... Didn't.

Interrogator: Speak, you animal!

Me: I am innocent, sir.

Interrogator: Liar!

Me: I...

Interrogator: You are not ready yet! Jailer!

One becomes half a zombie because the other half should remain a concious slave to amuse the captors.

Torture in, torture out for about ten days. I can't feel pain, can't feel time.

I am looking at a man lying completely still, no matter how hard the jailer is hitting and whipping him. It's that guy who came with a bullet in his body! He is dead! The jailer is kicking and swearing at a dead body! He knows the man is dead, yet he's still swearing at his lifeless body! He then leaves the body in our cell. We live with the body for about 3 days.
Nothing is too much anymore.

We became so senseless about anything and everything.
We are plain and hopeless.

We don't exist.

Part VI. Breathe! (2011)
Conclusion

It's the middle of June

Jailer: Get that mule!
Jailer: Stand still, don't move you animal

slap

camera flash

Gosh, is that a camera?

Jailer: Move!

Blindfolded, handcuffed, dragged to interrogation.

Interrogator: We have researched you and checked your PC but found nothing.
We know you're a good man and you have nothing to do with that conspiracy.
The minister of Endowments is your relative, right?

I have no damn idea what the heck you're talking about.

Me: Umm... Yea, yes, of course, he is. He always taught us to respect and protect
this country with our blood.

Interrogator: I see. Is there anyone bothering you in jail?
Me: No no. The guys are really nice!
Interrogator: Well we are still discussing your case, I think we'll let you go
soon.

Is this some game?

Me: Thank you sir.
Interrogator: Jailer!

A few days go by, the torture becomes softer, which gave me hope that the last interrogator was not bluffing. Time becomes slower, more people join our cell and are tortured in front of me, it's getting really unbearable.

Few days after that ..

Oh! No! Is this how I will lose my virginity?

I hear the sound of a trimming machine, and it's the second worst thing I was afraid of. They want to cut my hair after all these weeks of being the only detainee with remarkably long hair. The trimming machine is old and rusty and dull. The machine is getting stuck in my hair.

Gosh the pain!

The jailer takes me to a room, with lots of files on a desk. Someone is writing stuff on a piece of paper. The paper is covered with stamps and attached to it is a mugshot of a severely dishevelled man. I stare at the photo. That guy looks so fucked up and weary. Long beard, dirty face and... Hey! Wait a minute! That's me! Oh my God! It is me! I didn't recognize myself! I look so different, I forgot how I looked!

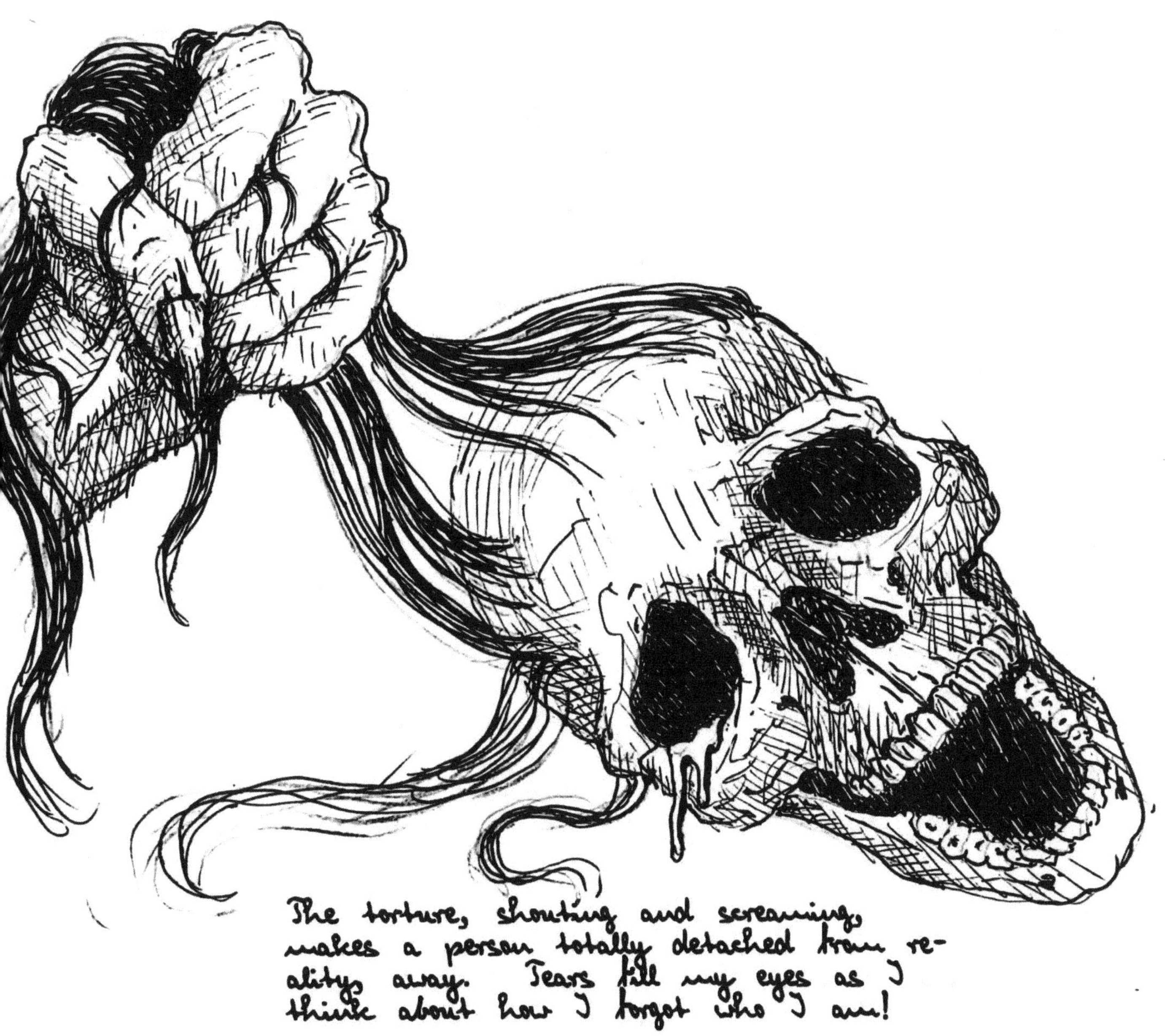

The torture, shouting and screaming, makes a person totally detached from reality away. Tears fill my eyes as I think about how I forgot who I am!

Jailer: Zymolust Ravenson! Get here you idiot. Move. Sign here, and fuck off.

I'm in the reception now, with the same guy who hit me when I got in.

Him: Is this your wallet?

Me: Yes, sir.

Him: Here, take your belongings, and sign this form. Well, that's everything, right?

Son of a...! They stole my money and my leather belt!

Me: Umm, there was some money in it. You know sir, I need to get home. Also my belt.

Him: Let me check. There is nothing, maybe the guys needed that belt. It's ok.

It's not a big deal. And about your money, you know, just thank your God you're out.

Me: Yes, of course, it's not a big deal sir. No problem at all.

Him: Also thank the great President Bashar Al-Assad

May God burn him in a special place in hell!

Me: May God put him in a special place in paradise.

Him: Amen.

Amen! You son of a bitch!

Me: Ameen! Dear sir.

I am taken in that same disgusting white Peugeot out of that hell just 100 meters away from that building. I am out! I am standing on the sidewalk!

Breathe..
It's real...

Now, I'm in the middle of the street on a sidewalk. Filthy, randomly trimmed hair, no money, somewhere in Damascus. Not to mention my cellphone was taken from me back in Tartous before all this.

-Do you think I should stop someone and ask them where the hell I am?
-Yes. Why not also ask them what year it is? At least you don't have to ask who the president is.
-I don't know what to do.
-Let's just stop a taxi and ask the driver.
-I like this amazing idea. You're one of a kind!

SO STOP A GODDAMN TAXI!

So I stop a taxi.

Me: Hey, can I ask you something, it might sound a bit weird

Driver: Sure.

Me: Umm, where is here? Where am I?

Driver: Hahaha... It's Kafr Sousa – Damascus. Are you lost?

- Katar What?

Me: Would you take me to Tartous? I'll give you any money when we're there, no discussion. Deal?

Driver: Deal!

- Wow! That was easy.
- Don't you think we should've haggled for a price?
- I'm really not used to this.
- Just to have an Ide...
- GET THE FUCK OUTA HERE!
- YES!

I'm in the taxi heading to Tartous. I'm out... I'm free! I'm home. My parents can't believe I am back. They literally didn't know where I was. For them I was lost. I talk to mom, explain to her that there are two options, either you don't see me whilst I'm in one of Assad's hells, or you don't see me while I'm abroad in some country.

Me: I hate this country, Mom. I just can't take this hell anymore. I want to die somewhere else.

Mom: I understand. Just be okay.

Next thing I'm out of this goddamn hell called Syria within 48 hours once and for all. I decided to fight this hell with writing.

Assad committed crimes against humanity yet he tears us still.

Words are our only weapon, and so there you go!